Porn and You

Joshua Wong

Porn and You
ISBN-13: 978-1495459610
ISBN-10: 1495459616
Copyright © 2014 by Joshua Wong

Contents

Introduction

> By the way, pornography? It's a new synaptic path-
> way. You wake up in the morning, open a thumb-
> nail page, and it leads to a Pandora's box of visu-
> als. There have probably been days when I saw 300
> vaginas before I got out of bed.

> – John Mayer[1]

What is pornography? While we believe it is a term that needs no precise or full definition for one to actually know what it means, it is nonetheless useful for us to define this term as a basis for talking about it in this book. We may define pornography as any material that is "predominantly sexually explicit and intended primarily for the purpose of sexual arousal", per the 1986 Attorney General Commission on Pornography.

Porn is currently distributed via every media conceivable. The most common and easily available porn is distributed via

---

[1] http://www.playboy.com/playground/view/playboy-interview-john-mayer?page=2

the internet. These may include so called "tube sites", named for their similarity to YouTube, where anonymous users may upload their own content (mostly pirated), subscription-based porn sites managed by porn studios, and "live" webcam sites where sex workers can interact in real time with their customers.

Porn is also distributed via magazines (such as Playboy, or Penthouse). These are available easily at adult bookstores. Because such magazines do not violate the law's standard of obscenity, they can be legally distributed. Another form of distribution, through video cassettes, is common. Such videos typically show hard-core porn, and depict extremely explicit or even illegal content. Some people may consider R rated movies shown at cinema theaters as pornographic too. With the normalization of porn in our culture, what would have been considered pornographic by our parents is now shown at cinemas without much objection.

The amount of porn consumed just over the internet is staggering. According to one report, people have watched 1.2 million years of porn since 2006 on just two popular porn tube sites.[2] According to Ogi Ogas, "in 2010, out of the million most popular (most trafficked) websites in the world, 42,337 were sex-related sites. That's about 4% of sites. From July 2009 to July 2010, about 13% of Web searches were for erotic content."[3]

---

[2]http://readwrite.com/2012/12/18/12-million-years-of-porn-watched-since—2006-on-just—2-tube-sites#awesm=~ojhScfFjdw2W2D

[3]http://www.forbes.com/sites/julieruvolo/2011/09/07/how-much-of-the-internet-is-actually-for-porn/

The kinds (or genres) of porn available are too numerous to enumerate, and covers the whole range of human sexual behavior from non-violent, non-degrading porn to what most would find repulsive and illegal, such as child porn. As porn becomes more widely and easily available via the internet, it shouldn't surprise anyone that it is likely that teenagers and more technologically savvy users of the internet would be more likely to consume not just more porn, but a wider range of porn.

Part One of this book will discuss the various ways porn is harmful. In Chapter One, we will look at how regular consumption of porn is likely to harm a person's ability to enjoy sex in real life. Porn causes dissatisfaction in relationships and has even destroyed marriages.

Chapter Two will look at how the "pornification" of society is likely to lead to increasingly earlier exposure to porn by our young. Young persons are increasingly using the internet to seek out porn, and may at times even cross the line and delve into illegal content such as child porn. Apart from upsetting young children who are still maturing sexually, porn also distorts their expectations of sex and leads to earlier sexual participation and violent or non-mainstream sexual behavior.

Chapter Three will look at how porn is bad for those who work in the industry as performers. Apart from the clear health risks that they face, many performers also experience physical and psychological abuse. This is a direct consequence of the direction in porn towards themes of violence and humiliation. Performers in porn also frequently find themselves unable to maintain long term romantic relationships due to the nature of their work.

In Part Two, we will be looking at how a person can go porn free. Chapter Four will help you determine if a person has an addiction to porn, and help to identify the extent and causes of that addiction. It is valuable to be able to differentiate between addiction on a physical level and addiction on a deeper psychological level.

Chapter Five covers two categories of triggers that would lead a person to consume porn. Triggers can be made up of any event, situation, or scenario that first plants the idea in a person's mind of porn. Effective management of an addiction to porn involves the correct identification of the first exact moment where porn comes to mind. We will be discussing Environmental and Situational triggers.

In Chapter Six, we will talk two effective strategies that a person can use to deal with porn addiction: Cold-Turkey and Community-Accountability. An awareness of the triggers would allow a person to completely stop looking at porn long enough that the brain can recover. By getting what we call an Accountability Partner, a person would also find support from someone who is going through the same struggles and mutually help each other break free from porn.

The Appendix will point you to further resources that are useful for someone looking to cut porn out from their lives.

Part I

Harmful effects of porn

Chapter 1

Porn harms you

Porn today

Porn is today ubiquitously available via the internet and the development of new technologies.

Just 30 years ago, one would not expect to be able to access hundreds or even thousands of pornographic images or videos at once. The primary way of consuming porn was via printed materials or videos with at most tens of images. With broadband internet becoming more widely available, anyone with a computer, smartphone, or laptop can reach porn at the click of a button. Such a widespread availability of porn has been claimed to alter the way we respond to sex in real life.

The internet has also contributed to the economics of porn by making it economically viable to shoot and distribute even niche genres of porn to cater to all kinds of fetishes. According to the theory of the long tail, the internet allows millions of niche markets to exist by enabling people to easily discover and satisfy even the narrowest of their interests. Traditionally, retail economics would prescribe that distribution channels only stock products that were acceptable to the mass market. Products that only appeal to niche markets would not be so attractive to stock due to a small local market. However, the long tail of the market, that is, the potential aggregate size of the demand for all these small niche markets might make it commercially attractive to cater to. This explains the proliferation of porn genres, and can be seen as a driving factor in the creation of ever more shocking and illegal content.

The most popular adult site on the web today is LiveJasmin, a webcam site where men can pay to watch women strip while talking to them. This innovation in porn distribution is made possible with the cheap availability of computer cameras, broadband access, and completely redefines the kinds of pornographic content available today. According to Ogi Ogas, "The fact that 2.5% of the billion people on the Internet are using LiveJasmin each month is pretty extraordinary." Just a decade ago, such levels of interactivity in porn would have been unthinkable.

Porn producers and studios have always been early adopters of technology. According to Patchen Barss, author of "The Erotic Engine: How Pornography has Powered Mass Communication from Gutenberg to Google",

> From cave painting to photography to the internet, pornography has always been at the cutting

edge in adopting and exploiting new developments in mass communication. And in so doing, it has helped to promote and propel those developments in ways that are rarely acknowledged. Without pornography, the internet would not have grown so quickly. The e-commerce payment systems that are now commonplace would be at a far more primitive stage security and usability. Without video streaming software developed for pornography sites, CNN would be struggling to deliver news clips. Without advertising from sex sites, Google could not have afforded YouTube.

With the invention of new technologies such as 3D video, Google Glass, it is likely that consumption of porn will become more immersive and pervasive in the long term. With the porn industry developing new technologies such as computer controlled sex toys[1] it is not difficult to see how porn consumption might become even more interactive and engaging, with consequently higher rates of its attendant problems.

It should be clear that there is a trend towards ever increasing consumption of porn in our society. Not only is there an increasingly wider availability of porn, the kinds of porn that one might consume is also likely to proliferate. With the adoption of new technologies which provide more immersive and

---

[1]Apparently known as teledildonics. http://www.businessinsider.com.au/how-porn-drives-innovation-in-tech–2013–7

interactive experiences, one might imagine a nation of masturbators spending more time on porn and less time on real life relationships.

Porn harms your brain

When a person consumes porn, it directly messes with his/her brain, leading to changes that are very hard to reverse. As porn becomes more visceral and hardcore today, the magnitude of changes in the brain of a porn consumer is accordingly getting higher and more deep-rooted. Research into the functioning of our brains by neuroscientists is beginning to explain how porn works to make us ever more dependent on seeking it out. It rewires our brains and then proceeds to harm our sex in real life.

According to psychiatrist Norman Doidge, porn possesses the full recipe for causing neuroplastic change in us, and he explains why porn can lead to a rewiring of our brains:[2]

> Pornography is more exciting than satisfying because we have two separate pleasure systems in our brains, one that has to do with exciting pleasure and one with satisfying pleasure. The exciting system relates to the "appetitive" pleasure that we get imagining something we desire, such as

[2]Extract from Doidge, N. (2007). The brain that changes itself: Stories of personal triumph from the frontiers of brain science.

sex or a good meal. Its neurochemistry is largely dopamine-related, and it raises our tension level.

The second pleasure system has to do with the satisfaction, or consummatory pleasure, that attends actually having sex or having that meal, a calming, fulfilling pleasure. Its neurochemistry is based on the release of endorphins, which are related to opiates and give a peaceful, euphoric bliss.

Pornography, by offering an endless harem of sexual objects, hyperactivates the appetitive system. Porn viewers develop new maps in their brains, based on the photos and videos they see. Because it is a use-it-or-lose-it brain, when we develop a map area, we long to keep it activated. Just as our muscles become impatient for exercise if we've been sitting all day, so too do our senses hunger to be stimulated.

The men at their computers looking at porn were uncannily like the rats in the cages of the NIH, pressing the bar to get a shot of dopamine or its equivalent. Though they didn't know it, they had been seduced into pornographic training sessions that met all the conditions required for plastic change of brain maps. Since neurons that fire together wire together, these men got massive amounts of practice wiring these images into the pleasure centers of the brain, with the rapt attention necessary for plastic change. They imagined these images when away from their computers, or while having sex with their girlfriends, reinforcing them. Each time they felt sexual excitement and had an orgasm when they masturbated, a "spritz of dopamine," the reward neurotransmitter, consolidated the connections made in the brain during the sessions. Not only did the reward facilitate the behavior; it provoked none of the embarrassment they felt purchasing Playboy at a store. Here was a behavior with no "punishment," only reward.

The content of what they found exciting changed as the Web sites introduced themes and scripts that altered their brains without their awareness. Because plasticity is competitive, the brain maps for new, exciting images increased at the expense of what had previously attracted them—the reason, I believe, they began to find their girlfriends less of a turn-on.

The problem with porn, then, is that it progressively sucks you into a pattern of addiction by rewiring your brain to enjoy certain "themes or scripts" which you cannot possibly satisfy in real life. The more you consume porn videos and pictures, the more your brain would crave activation of your appetitive system, and the more you would seek out more hardcore porn that you might have previously considered off-limits.

Porn harms you

As porn rewires your brain, it becomes a substitute for what turned you on in real life previously, with troubling outcomes such as the inability to enjoy sex with your partner. You might start to have trouble being aroused by your partner, and might start to fantasize about porn sex even when having real sex.

The story of Sean Thomas, as recounted in Norman Doidge's book, The Brain That Changes Itself: Stories of Personal Triumph from the Frontiers of Brain Science,[3] is quite the vivid account:

> But in 2001, shortly after he first went online, he got curious about the porn everyone said was taking over the Internet. Many of the sites were free—teasers, or "gateway sites," to get people into the harder stuff. There were galleries of naked girls, of common types of sexual fantasies and attractions, designed to press a button in the brain of the surfer, even one he didn't know he had. There were pictures of lesbians in a Jacuzzi, cartoon porn, women on the toilet smoking, coeds, group sex, and men ejaculating over submissive Asian women. Most of the pictures told a story.
>
> Thomas found a few images and scripts that appealed to him, and they "dragged me back for more the next day. And the next. And the next." Soon

---

[3]Doidge, N. (2007). The brain that changes itself: Stories of personal triumph from the frontiers of brain science.

he found that whenever he had a spare minute, he would "start hungrily checking out Net Porn."

Then one day he came across a site that featured spanking images. To his surprise, he got intensely excited. Thomas soon found all sorts of related sites, such as "Bernie's Spanking Pages" and the "Spanking College."

"This was the moment," he writes, "that the real addiction set in. My interest in spanking got me speculating: What other kinks was I harboring? What other secret and rewarding corners lurked in my sexuality that I would now be able to investigate in the privacy of my home? Plenty, as it turned out. I discovered a serious penchant for, inter alia, lesbian gynecology, interracial hardcore, and images of Japanese girls taking off their hotpants. I was also into netball players with no knickers, drunk Russian girls exposing themselves, and convoluted scenarios where submissive Danish actresses were intimately shaved by their dominant female partners in the shower. The Net had, in other words, revealed to me that I had an unquantifiable variety of sexual fantasies and quirks and that the process of satisfying these desires online only led to more interest."

This story is familiar. Males start off stumbling onto some pornographic sites, and they start to return to it on a regular basis. After prolonged periods of surfing porn, they find themselves requiring more and more visual stimulation and more hardcore porn to excite them. Coupled with curiosity and the easy availability of all kinds of fetish sites online, they start to venture into material that would have previously shocked them. Due to the rewiring of their neural circuits and the reinforcing nature of porn induced orgasms, they find that the excitement and pleasure of novel material has overwritten their initial disgust of these more shocking material.

Another way porn keeps you coming back for more has to do with how we experience pleasure and how our brain regulates how much pleasure we experience from our activities, such as sex, eating, and exercise.

Sensors in our brains, called dopamine receptors, light up whenever our brain releases dopamine. Basically, there are two ways that we can increase our levels of pleasure. One way would be to get our brain to release more dopamine. Have more sex, eat more food. For example, cocaine works by increasing the amount of dopamine in the brain, which causes the drug high.

Another way would be to increase the number of dopamine receptors that can translate the dopamine released into the sensation of pleasure. This is actually not likely to happen though. In reality, it seems that our receptors start to switch off once they are exposed to a surge of dopamine, which, as we'll see later, causes us to require more and more of the same to experience the equivalent amount of pleasure.

How does your brain release dopamine? It's released whenever you anticipate a reward coming along or whenever you engage in something enjoyable. For example, getting a promotion at work, achieving a personal goal, scoring an A in an exam, or winning a game. Why would your brain do such a thing? It releases dopamine so that you feel good whenever you do something which your brain identifies as improving your survival (or your genetic fitness). Eating great food, achieving something important, winning a game, or having sex are all accompanied by dopamine surges (whether according to the anticipatory hypothesis or the pleasure hypothesis). In turn, your dopamine receptors start working and you experience pleasure.[4]

When we repeatedly surf porn, our brain gets increasingly used to the stimulation, and the anticipation of the pleasure gets correspondingly numbed. When that happens, our brain does not need to release any more dopamine to signal to you that you are about to experience another sexual high. In an experiment, scientists rewarded monkeys with juice for successfully completing a task. At the beginning of the experiment, the measured dopamine levels of the monkeys surged with every reward, but as they continued getting the same rewards, their brains started to stop responding to them, and their dopamine levels dropped. Translated into human terms, once we are habituated to certain rewards, our brain starts to take these rewards for granted, and starts to focus on other new forms of rewards. In short, the

---

[4]In an interesting article, reporters claimed that eating cupcakes could cause so much dopamine to hit the brain that it is as likely to be as addictive as cocaine. Read it at http://www.thesun.co.uk/sol/homepage/woman/health/3913703/Are-cupcakes-as-addictive-as-cocaine.html

more we think we are having sex, the more the brain stops caring about sex, and the less satisfying sex becomes.

Dopamine surges might also actually also lead to us being unable to experience pleasure overall by shutting down our dopamine pleasure receptors. The striatal dopamine D2 receptors tend to get "downregulated" in humans with drug addiction problems, who then have to seek out even more drugs to reach the same levels of high. The striatum is associated with our decision making system, and is activated by stimuli associated with reward, but also by aversive, novel, unexpected, or intense stimuli, and cues associated with such events. In the case of drug consumption, a cascade of dopamine floods the brain and causes the high. When this happens, the receptors in the brain reacts by shutting down, which ends the euphoric effect of the drug.

In extreme cases of bingeing leading to an uprush of dopamine production, our receptors start to shut down completely for a long period. For instance, in a widely cited study, cocaine abusers experienced a remarkable dwindling of their dopamine D2 receptor availability which lasted for three to four months after detoxification.[5]

When we experience unnaturally high levels of pleasure brought about by bingeing on porn, our ability to enjoy pleasure deteriorates, and not just for a few days, but for weeks or

---

[5]Volkow, N. D., Fowler, J. S., Wang, G. J., Hitzemann, R., Logan, J., Schlyer, D. J., ... & Wolf, A. P. (1993). Decreased dopamine D2 receptor availability is associated with reduced frontal metabolism in cocaine abusers. Synapse, 14(2), 169–177.

13

even months. In other studies, dopamine receptor downregulation has been hypothesized as the reason why obese people continue to overeat.[6] In a vicious cycle, overeating causes the pleasure from food to weaken, causing even more overeating and increased obesity.

The same effect applies to the consumption of porn. Due to the constant surge in dopamine when we binge on porn hours at a time, our brain starts to react by shutting down our pleasure receptors. This explains why porn becomes less pleasurable and more addictive: the more we seek it out, the less it does for us, and yet the more we continue to seek it out.

To sum it all up, porn draws us into consuming more and more of it by rewiring our brains' circuitry to take pleasure in what we previously would not have enjoyed. In addition, by hijacking the pleasure response system of our brains, it induces us to seek out more and more of it to compensate for its dulling effect.

It would be fair to suggest that no one is actually naturally inclined to enjoy child or bestiality porn. However, the reinforcing nature of porn has led some people down the slippery slope of progressing from softcore porn to porn that they would never have expected to have turned them on. If this seems to describe your behavior, you might be thinking of how you can possibly change. In Part Two of this book, we suggest some

---

[6]Stice, E., Spoor, S., Bohon, C., Veldhuizen, M. G., & Small, D. M. (2008). Relation of reward from food intake and anticipated food intake to obesity: a functional magnetic resonance imaging study. Journal of abnormal psychology, 117(4), 924.

ways to help you overcome the effects of porn on your brain. To that end, perhaps some more words from the same Norman Doidge as quoted above would be reassuring:

> for the patients who became involved in porn, most were able to go cold turkey once they understood the problem and how they were plastically reinforcing it. They found eventually that they were attracted once again to their mates. None of these men had addictive personalities or serious childhood traumas, and when they understood what was happening to them, they stopped using their computers for a period to weaken their problematic neuronal networks, and their appetite for porn withered away.

Porn causes erectile dysfunction

In order to understand how porn can harm males' ability to have erections, we have to delve a little into the science of erections. What is the purpose of your penis? (we shall assume a male reader in this section) Basically your penis has two functions. The first is as a way for your body to release urine from your bladder. This is the most commonly used function of the penis. The second is the release of sperm produced in your testes and seminal fluid from your prostate gland during sex. Typically, ejaculations are accompanied by orgasms.

Some interesting facts about your penis. While there are no bones in your penis, it can nonetheless be "broken". During an erection, if you or your partner is not careful, the tubes that fill with blood in your penis can break, causing blood to swell in your penis. This is how an article describes it: "It's what we call penile fracture. It is a severe form of bending injury to the erect penis that occurs when a membrane called the tunica albuginea tears. The tunica albuginea surrounds the corpora cavernosa, specialized spongy tissue in the core of the penis that fills up with blood during an erection. When the tunica albuginea tears, the blood that is normally confined to this space leaks out into other tissues. You get bruising and swelling."[7] An article in The Awl recounts the personal experience of someone who broke his penis during sex.[8]

Contrary to popular belief, your penis does not contain muscles. It is more like a sponge that swells when blood rushes in during an erection. An erect penis can thus be viewed as a pressure powered device. One way to look at it is to imagine it as a balloon. Limp when there's no air in it, it becomes large, taut, and hard when you blow air into it. During an erection, instead of air, your body quickly pumps pressurized blood from your arteries into your penis through two tubes,[9] which expands to hold up to 90 percent of the blood involved with the erection. The veins that are normally open during a non-erect state

[7] http://www.scientificamerican.com/article.cfm?id=can-you-really-break-your

[8] The Time I Broke It. http://www.theawl.com/2012/03/the-incident-report-or-the-time-i-broke-it

[9] These are called corpora cavernosa, literally "cave-like bodies".

start to constrict, and the pressurized blood in your penis keeps the penis erect. To protect your urethra and prevent it from compression, it is housed within another tube called the corpus spongiosum.

How does the body know when to turn on the valves and pump pressurized blood into your penis? When you are aroused, your brain sends a signal to your arteries and penis to instruct them to relax. When relaxed, blood flow increases. However, at the same time, the chemicals which tell your arteries to relax get deactivated by another chemical, and unless the brain continually sends instructions to your arteries, your erection quickly subsides due to the deactivation of the chemicals which tell your penis to become erect.

There are multiple points of failure in your erection system. For one, if your brain doesn't register anything as sexually arousing, it will never send any instructions to your penis, and you will never get an erection. Also, certain individuals may have poor blood flow due to health problems that causes insufficient blood to reach the penis for an erection. An erection can also be difficult to sustain if the chemicals which maintain the erection get deactivated too quickly.

Coupled with the discussion earlier on how our brain eventually habituates to porn and needs more and more of it to release the same amount of dopamine, you can begin to understand how porn can lead to the onset of erectile dysfunctions. For instance, your brain might register real life sexual encounters as not as arousing as online porn, and hence fail to send instructions to your penis to create an erection. The numbing of your arousal system causes you to suffer from an inability to sustain an erection for real life sex.

While it is not usual for the elderly to report an inability to sustain an erection due to old age, legions of healthy men in their twenties and thirties are now suffering from porn induced erectile dysfunction. This in itself should not be surprising—compared to the legions of "super hot" porn stars who are willing to do anything on the screen, ordinary real life sex can start to pale in comparison. It is no wonder that habitual porn consumption can so overwhelm our brains' pleasure response patterns that we no longer find real life sex appealing.

Porn causes delayed ejaculation

Masturbation is still more or less considered a taboo subject, and is rarely brought up in public discussions. In the past, people thought that masturbation would lead to blindness, cause impotency, or even that it would cause hair to grow on the palms of one's hands. In fact, masturbation was seen as such an evil in the past that John Harvey Kellogg called it "a crime doubly abominable". This was the same Kellogg who invented corn flakes as "healthy, ready-to-eat anti-masturbatory morning meals."[10]

Today, while the topic of masturbation is still considered off limits in polite society, it is generally accepted as something

---

[10]http://mentalfloss.com/article/32042/corn-flakes-were-invented-part-anti-masturbation-crusade

everyone does. Surveys indicate that up to 95 percent of men and 71 percent of women have masturbated at some point in their lives. While masturbation is considered a normal behavior, porn has altered the way we masturbate. Most men use porn as an aid to masturbation, and almost all men masturbate while watching porn. Because porn is so easily available, and consumption of it so addictive, men easily go into a pattern of compulsive behavioral pattern of excessive porn aided masturbation. This creates serious problems for regular porn masturbators, including delayed ejaculation or in the worst case, an inability to reach orgasm at all, a condition called anorgasmia.

Porn encourages excessive masturbation through a process known as the Coolidge Effect. What is the Coolidge Effect? It is a phenomenon seen in nature where males are more likely to be willing and able to mate with new females even though they have already lost interest in prior sexual partners.

> an old joke about Calvin Coolidge when he was President...The President and Mrs. Coolidge were being shown [separately] around an experimental government farm. When [Mrs. Coolidge] came to the chicken yard she noticed that a rooster was mating very frequently. She asked the attendant how often that happened and was told, "Dozens of times each day." Mrs. Coolidge said, "Tell that to the President when he comes by." Upon being told, President asked, "Same hen every time?" The reply was, "Oh, no, Mr. President, a differ-

ent hen every time." President: "Tell that to Mrs. Coolidge."[11]

In an experiment, a male rat was allowed to mate with four or five female rats in estrus. After repeatedly mating with all the female rats, he eventually became exhausted and unable to mate anymore, despite the females' continued encouragement. However, when a new female rat was introduced, he began to mate again with the new female.

With reference to our discussion above, this behavior can been attributed to the rise of dopamine which accompanies the availability of a new female. After mating repeatedly with the same female, the brain stops producing dopamine when faced with the prospect of more sex with the same mate. Dopamine production is only triggered when a new sexual partner is available, as mating with the new female would increase the likelihood of procreating more offspring.

Does this effect apply to humans? Human males experience a refractory period after ejaculation, and are unable to engage in sex again for some time. This period can last from a few minutes to days, depending on age, health, and the frequency of sexual activity. However, when a new female is available, this period is reduced or even eliminated. In other words, while a human male might be unable to have sex with the same woman immediately after sex, introduce another female willing to have

---

[11]Hatfield, E., & Walster, G. W. (1978). A new look at love. University Press of America.

sex with him and the chances are high that he will be able to get an erection and have sex with the new female.

In most of mankind's history, males normally did not have access to more than a handful of sexually receptive females at a time. Today, porn has changed all that. When surfing porn, our brains are fooled into thinking that there are hundreds upon hundreds of sexually available partners, and the Coolidge effect kicks in. As we click on from one image to another, our brains are fooled into thinking there are more females/males available for us to have sex with. Porn puts us in an unnaturally long and intense state of sexual stimulation.

For instance, you could be surfing porn and masturbating at the same time, and because novel images and videos come up all the time, you end up masturbating for hours before you reach orgasm. This quote from John Mayer in a Playboy Magazine interview should give you a good idea of what many men who regularly consume porn experience: "You're looking for the one photo out of 100 you swear is going to be the one you finish to, and you still don't finish. Twenty seconds ago you thought that photo was the hottest thing you ever saw, but you throw it back and continue your shot hunt and continue to make yourself late for work."[12]

After years of porn use, many men experience delayed ejaculation problems as a result of the Coolidge effect conditioning themselves to only orgasm after a long time masturbating to porn. In addition to delayed ejaculation, many men also find

---

[12]http://www.playboy.com/playground/view/playboy-interview-john-mayer?page=2

that they are unable to orgasm at all while having sex with their partners.

Another reason why masturbating to porn might cause delayed ejaculation is that excessive masturbation can destroy the sensitive nerve endings in our sex organs. In a sex advice column written by Dan Savage, a reader asks the following question:[13]

> Remember how one time (or maybe two) you warned a guy (while remaining masturbation-positive) not to condition his body to come only in response to a particular kind of stimulation? I believe ('cause I looked 'em up) your exact words were, "If you hold your cock in a death grip every time, you may find it difficult to climax as the result of other, more subtle sensations."
>
> Well, unfortunately, I read your excellent advice too late. About 30 years too late. So now, while women think it's cool that I can "stay hard all night," they eventually start to get a complex about the fact that, though they're having orgasms galore, they can't seem to make me come. It's not them, of course. It's the years and years and years of death-grip masturbation.
>
> Help me, Dan. What can I do to climax in response to "more subtle sensations"?

_____
[13]http://www.thestranger.com/seattle/
Content?oid=14968&mode=print

Porn harms you

A Big Fan

Due to years of masturbating with what the letter writer terms a "death-grip" he finds himself unable to respond to real life sex.

When masturbating to porn, due to the intense nature of the pornographic images and videos available, men might apply too much force and take such a long time to reach orgasm that their penis gets chafed. When men masturbate for an extended period of time, the friction between the penis and the hand might start to cause parts of the skin on the penis to abrade away, causing temporary or permanent damage: bleeding, dryness, and even damage to the nerve endings. This might also occur when men masturbate with objects (such as with socks) which introduce excessive and unnecessary friction or during prolonged penile-vaginal intercourse.

Over a period of time, excessive masturbation conditions the penis to only respond to rough sensations, due to both psychological reasons and physical wear and tear. In extreme cases, it might be the case that the physical damage is so extensive that there is no longer any cure. Dan Savage replied to the reader as follows:

> Your problem may not be fixable, because your dick, after 30 years of abuse, may be too far gone. If that's the case, you may have to accept your fate, adjust, and deal.

Excessive masturbation and porn consumption is thus likely to cause problems of delayed ejaculation and might even lead to an inability to reach orgasm through penile-vaginal intercourse.

Porn harms your relationships

Consider the case of John and Jane, a married couple of seven years. After years of marriage, the couple stopped having regular intercourse after Jane had her second pregnancy two years ago. Every night, her husband would spend hours on the internet consuming hardcore porn and masturbating, and would not initiate sex at all, claiming that he was exhausted. Jane eventually found out about her husband's porn habit when porn sites started popping up on the family computer and she went through her husband's browsing history.

Apart from feeling hurt that John was lying to her about his porn addiction, she felt as though her husband had cheated on her, leading to an erosion of trust and a deep sense of disappointment.

A study of 531 internet users in 2000 concluded that there was a strong predictive effect of the use of porn on marriage happiness (the more porn use, the lower the marriage happiness).[14] Happily married couples are 61 percent less likely to report the use of porn. In addition, it concluded that porn users are 3.1 times more likely to have an extramarital affair and 3.7 times more likely to have visited prostitutes.

This is not surprising. Porn makes "real life" sex seem unexciting by contrast, and creates an appetite for a perverse kind of sex which cannot be fulfilled in a marriage. It is likely to erode

---

[14]Stack, S., Wasserman, I., & Kern, R. (2004). Adult Social Bonds and Use of Internet Pornography*. Social science quarterly, 85(1), 75–88.

the level satisfaction even in healthy marriages, and worsen existing marriage problems.

In a related study by the same researchers studying the impact of porn consumption on attitudes towards marriage, the authors found that porn eroded peoples' attitudes on the importance of marriage.[15] Exposure to porn led to an increased acceptance of premarital sex and extramarital affairs, and made nonexclusive sexual access to other partners more acceptable. Indeed, porn frequently includes in its themes those of swinging, where partners in a committed relationship engage in sexual activities with others as a recreational or social activity, and cuckolding, a fetish where the fetishist is sexually stimulated by their committed partner choosing to have sex with someone else. Porn enhances the idea that promiscuity is natural and that the repression of sexual inclinations poses a health peril. According to this study, "Exposure [to pornography] also reduced the desire to have children and promoted the acceptance of male dominance and female servitude."

Consumption of porn has also been shown to lead to dissatisfaction with our sexual partners. In a study, research participants were exposed weekly to videos depicting either nonviolent porn or innocuous content.[16] After six weeks of such hourly videos, they were asked in the seventh week for their

---

[15]Zillmann, D., & Bryant, J. (1988). Effects of prolonged consumption of pornography on family values. Journal of Family Issues, 9(4), 518–544.

[16]Zillmann, D., & Bryant, J. (1988). Pornography's Impact on Sexual Satisfaction1. Journal of Applied Social Psychology, 18(5), 438–453.

views on a questionnaire on societal institutions and their personal life. Participants who were exposed to porn were strongly affected by it in their self-assessment of their sexual lives. In particular, they reported less satisfaction with their sexual partners, their affection, physical appearance, and even sexual performance. Participants exposed to porn also attached increased importance to casual sex and less importance to sex in committed relationships.

These studies give clear evidence that the use of porn is likely to lead to an increase in the breakdown of committed relationships, increasing the likelihood of extramarital affairs, casual relationships, and lower marital happiness. These findings also suggest the possibility that porn is the cause of divorces. In a recent study, divorce rates in the US were studied with the sales of Playboy magazine, with the authors concluding that sales of Playboy caused between 10 and 25 percent of all divorces in the US between 1962 and 1979.[17] By porn standards today, Playboy magazine is considered relatively mild compared to the explicit material easily available today on the internet. For Playboy to have caused up to one in four of all divorces 30 years ago is astounding, and should give pause to anyone considering the harmful effect of porn on marriages today.

---

[17]Daines, R. M., & Shumway, T. (2011). Pornography and Divorce.

Chapter 2

Porn harms children

Illegal porn

John (not real name) was just a child of ten years old when he first got introduced to porn. His friend introduced it to him. He was surprised that people could do such things with each other, and he felt strangely attracted to the images on his computer screen. For the next few years, he started going on to porn sites for hours daily to satisfy his curiosity while his parents didn't have a clue to what he was up to. They thought he was using his computer for homework.

One day, the police came knocking on John's door, and it was then that his parents found out about his secret addiction. It turned out that the police found out that someone in the house was accessing child porn, and had to raid the house to gather more evidence and build their case. When they found out the perpetrator was only 13, they were shocked. At 13 years old, John finds himself put on a sex offender register even though he had never even kissed a girl.

The incidence of hardcore porn use amongst our young can be shocking. In a UK documentary called Porn On The Brain, sex education consultant Jonny Hunt asked children on the show to write a list of all the sexual terms they knew. What he learnt shocked even him. Among the responses received from the kids, some barely prepubescent, were terms that even the adults did not know. For instance, one boy wrote the word "nugget", and when asked what it meant, happily replied that "a nugget is a girl who has no arms or legs and has sex in a porno movie". The adults were appalled that not only does such porn actually exist, but that a 14 year old boy might have actually watched it.

Young people are particularly susceptible to unknowingly cross the line and delve into illegal material. Before puberty, children are more likely to be unaware of what are normal sexual boundaries and would not have established the ability to discriminate between what is healthy and unhealthy behavior. They might even have a prior "dirty" image of sex, and be surprised to find out that genitals and the region "down there" are not only used for urination and defecation, but also serve a sexual purpose. Due to their sexual immaturity and curiosity, everything depicted by porn seems equally foreign to them, and it is no wonder that they are more likely than even adults to consume porn which depict sexual practices outside common cultural and even legal norms.

Cases similar to John's are on the rise, as evidenced by the increasing case load of counsellors and social workers who work with teenagers and children on issues of sexuality, shame, and their confusion between real life and the fantasy world of porn. For instance, in just a year, there have been 50 referrals to therapists of children under 18 for porn related sexual dysfunctions in London. According to a therapist, boys as young as 12 have been referred to her after they received convictions for looking at child porn and not realizing that it was illegal. In another case, a 13 year old boy sexually abused his five year old sister due to his confusion between his fantasy world and real life.

Porn upsets children

Before the explosion of internet porn about 15 years ago, hardcore porn usually referred to any explicit depiction of intercourse between two individuals, with genitals shown, and softcore porn usually denoted images of women in various states of undress, breast exposed. Today, hardcore porn refers to images and videos involving themes of violence, coercion, exploitation, or humiliation. The themes of hardcore porn are now those of perversion, such as violent double vaginal and anal penetration, ejaculations on women's faces, and defecation/urination. Softcore porn is now what hardcore porn was years ago, and what was softcore porn can now be easily found in mainstream media—a widespread pornification of popular culture.

In the past, when porn was mainly distributed by magazines, stores would at least refuse to sell pornographic materials to underage teenagers and kids. Today, porn can be found easily, and can sometimes even pop-up inadvertently when browsing non-sex related sites, such as on peer-to-peer file sharing sites for downloading music, games, and files. Such sites are popular among the young and are funded by online advertisements. Banner ads and pop-up ads frequently appear on these sites, showing salacious images of women and inviting you to, for instance, "chat with girls on cam".

A growing number of studies point to the fact that large numbers of teenagers and children, particularly boys, are growing up in the presence of softcore porn (nudity, clothed sex) in the media, and exposed to hardcore porn online either inadvertently or deliberately. International surveys suggest that the rate of deliberate online porn consumption amongst minors ranges from about 10 percent to 30 percent. In two surveys conducted in 2000 and 2005, researchers found that more than one-third of minors report unsolicited exposure to sexual content online in the second survey, compared to 25 percent in the first survey, an increase of 9 percent.[1] Apart from online porn exposure, children are also exposed to porn in other media, such as television shows, music videos, or cinema movies.

Hardcore porn has found even found its way into video games played mostly by teenagers and young adults. For example, the video game Grand Theft Auto: San Andreas triggered widespread controversy when it was discovered that it was possible for players to access and control a sex scene in the

---

[1]Finkelhor, D., Mitchell, K., & Wolak, J. (2007). Online Victimization of Youth: Five Years Later.

game. In the latest version of the game, Grand Theft Auto V, an uncensored sex scene is part of the gameplay. This game was highly successful, generating more than $800 million in revenue within 24 hours of release. While given a rating of Mature 17+, it is likely that many teenagers and even children play it, given its wide popularity.

Children and teenagers report becoming extremely upset when exposed to porn accidentally. In a study, teenagers aged 11 to 17 related that porn dominated the list of things they found online which they found disgusting, describing their feelings as "repulsed", "upset", "sick", and "shocked". Girls are more likely to be troubled by porn than boys.

In the Belfast Telegraph, correspondent Lizi Patch shared her own story of how porn on the internet changed her 11 year old son's life.[2]

One of his new friends shared a video clip with him and he watched it as part of his efforts to fit in at his new secondary school. However, he had no idea what the clip would show: a women coerced into a savage and disgusting sexual act. Afterwards, she noticed her son becoming "sullen and easily upset". In a later conversation after dinner, her son confessed that he was nauseated by what he saw, could not stop thinking about it, and felt that his childhood was effectively over. According to her, "the degrading, shockingly violent porn...showed him a dark underbelly of an online world. Faced with this hideous new information, he simply doesn't know where to file it."

---

[2]http://www.belfasttelegraph.co.uk/opinion/news-analysis/the-day-porn-on-the-internet-changed-my-sons-life–29167921.html

As mainstream culture becomes "pornified" and online porn becomes more widely available, it is likely to have severe psychological effects on our children who stumble upon it before they are mature enough to process it. Despite the illegality of promoting pornographic materials to our young, the industry does not put in place any effective mechanism to block access to minors. About two-thirds percent of porn websites do not have adult-content warnings, and only a small minority of adult sites (about 3 percent) gate their content, requiring proof-of-age before allowing access.

The most widely used internet browsers, such as Firefox, Safari, Chrome, or Internet Explorer do not provide native filtering of age-inappropriate websites, and parents need to manually install family filter products to ensure that the internet is safe for their children.

Even when such services are installed, they are usually not effective, and the proliferation of sex sites means that it is an uphill task to prevent our children from accessing porn. With the increased use of smart devices such as iPhones and the ability for young people to easily share content with each other with their devices, it becomes almost a certainty that children would be exposed inadvertently to porn.

In the Appendix of this book, we recommend the most useful and effective internet filters and techniques.

Earlier sexual participation

While young people need to be educated on topics of sexuality, porn frequently presents a highly distorted view of sex, with its hardcore themes of violence and humiliation.

It has been demonstrated that regular and frequent consumption of porn by the young leads to them taking more liberal attitudes towards sex, and causes earlier sexual participation. A study of boys and girls from 12 to 14 years old demonstrated that exposure to porn or sexually explicit material was the strongest predictor of an increased likelihood of having had oral sex and sexual intercourse by middle adolescence (14 to 16 years old).[3]

Because porn depicts sex outside of any commitments, it is likely to encourage casual sexual encounters amongst our young. The current hookup culture, where teenagers choose to forgo dating totally in favor of casual hookups is symptomatic of the harm that porn is causing to our young. Studies show that it is common for high school students to have sex with someone they are not dating, and a survey in 2001 conducted by Bowling Green State University in Ohio found that of the 55 percent of local 11th graders (16 year olds) who engaged in intercourse, 60 percent said they'd had sex with a partner who was no more than a friend.

---

[3]Brown, J. D., & L'Engle, K. L. (2009). X-rated sexual attitudes and behaviors associated with US early adolescents' exposure to sexually explicit media. Communication Research, 36(1), 129–151.

Porn and You

By encouraging sexual behaviors at a young age, porn harms our children when it leads to emotional distress and unwanted teenage pregnancies. The story of Melissa, a high school senior, is common:[4]

> The day we met in person, Melissa was in a foul mood. Her "friend with benefits" had just broken up with her. "How is that even possible?" she said, sitting, shoulders slumped, in a booth at a diner. "The point of having a friend with benefits is that you won't get broken up with, you won't get hurt. He told me online that he met a girl that he really likes, so now, of course, we can't hook up anymore."

> "I have my friends for my emotional needs, so I don't need that from the guy I'm having sex with," Melissa explained at the time, sounding very much like the "Sex and the City" character Samantha Jones. So why, now that the boy had "broken up" with her, was she feeling so depressed? "It's really stupid, I know," she said, shaking her head. "It's kind of ironic, isn't it? I try to set up a situation where I won't get hurt, and I still manage to get hurt."

---

[4]Excerpted from Denizet-Lewis, B. (2004). Friends, friends with benefits and the benefits of the local mall. New York Times Magazine, 30, 1–9. http://www.nytimes.com/2004/05/30/magazine/friends-friends-with-benefits-and-the-benefits-of-the-local-mall.html?pagewanted=all&src=pm

Like other high-school girls I talked to, Melissa says she doesn't see why boys get to have "all the fun," although during the few months we communicated, it was clear that Melissa's hookups rarely brought her joy. She complained often about being depressed, and her hookups, which she hoped would make her feel better, usually left her feeling worse. But a few days after a hookup, she would have forgotten that they tended to make her miserable, and would tell me excitedly about a new boy she was planning to meet. When that boy failed to show or called to say he was running an hour late, Melissa's spirits would sink – again.

According to The National Campaign to Prevent Teen and Unplanned Pregnancy, boys are likely to rank porn equally with sex education when asked to rate their influences with regard to sex. Porn is clearly not a good way for teenagers to learn about sex. For instance, most internet porn do not feature the use of condoms, and may encourage the teenagers to disregard the use of contraceptives, leading to unwanted pregnancies. Among unmarried teenagers under the age of twenty, 70 in 100 pregnancies are unplanned, and the rates of teenage pregnancy in the US is one of the highest in the world, with almost 30 in 100 teenage girls under the age of twenty getting pregnant.

Non-mainstream sexual behavior

Porn leads to non-realistic expectations of sex by adolescents. Puberty is a critical period in our lives when we develop sexual maturity and our brains develop new maps for sexual behavior. When children and teenagers consume porn either during this critical period, it subverts their sexual maturation process, leading to lifelong sexual dysfunctions and the improper acceptance and adoption of non-mainstream sexual practices and attitudes. For instance, many women get confused today when their partners starts to request that they ejaculate on their faces, which is obviously degrading to women. However, men have been conditioned by porn to think that women actually enjoy it.

Porn consumption leads to increased male sexual aggressiveness in young people. In a study of 804 teenagers from the northwest of Italy, researchers found that "reading pornographic comics and magazines significantly increased the likelihood of having sexually harassed a peer or having forced somebody to have sex, while viewing pornographic films or videos increased the likelihood of being a victim of sexual violence."[5]

In one case, John (not real name), a young 18 year old man was referred to a counsellor by social workers who were worried that his addiction to porn made him a danger to others. According to an interview with his therapist, he reported that when a girl did not reciprocate his feelings, he felt "like stabbing

---

[5]Bonino, S., Ciairano, S., Rabaglietti, E., & Cattelino, E. (2006). Use of pornography and self-reported engagement in sexual violence among adolescents. European Journal of Developmental Psychology, 3(3), 265–288.

her". In addition, he felt suicidal over his fears of never being able to have a normal relationship.

The violent and coercive content of porn leads to greater tolerance towards sexually abusive attitudes. Porn contributes to the "rape myth" where boys grow up thinking that women enjoy sexual aggression. A study of 14 year old Canadian boys found that those who regularly consumed porn were more likely to agree that it is acceptable to hold a girl down and force her to have sex. Sexist views which objectify women as sexual objects are also regularly encouraged by hardcore porn.

Porn affects not only the attitudes of young males, but those of young females as well. Young girls may feel increased pressure from boys to replicate porn-like sexual behaviors, such as making out with other females to turn on their boyfriends or anal sex. Studies have found that Swedish young people who regularly consume porn were more likely to engage in anal sex. In addition, they might normalize abusive sexual relationships because they see the same acts committed in porn.

Sexting

A discussion of the impact of porn on our young would not be complete without a comment on a disturbing trend related to the proliferation of porn consumption among children and teenagers today.

Sexting is the act of sending sexually explicit messages and/or photographs, primarily between mobile phones, and has become a source of much anguish and pressure for teenagers. The phenomenon of sexting underlines the role of porn in redefining gender roles, the expectation of boys and girls in their relationships, and the danger that porn poses for our young. Intimately tied to this issue is the use of social networking sites and apps, which amplify the fallout from the consequences of unrealistic expectations created by porn consumption.

In a study published in 2013, the authors found that 20 in 100 participants of a high school have ever sent a sexually explicit picture of themselves by cell phone to others, and 40 in 100 participants had ever received a sexually explicit image.[6] Of these 40, over 10 of them indicated that they then forwarded such an image to others. This study highlighted the cavalier attitude that most teens have towards sharing sexual pictures of themselves and their peers with each other, despite knowing that sharing such images could be illegal and often lead to harmful consequences.[7]

A large majority of teenagers these days report being active on social networking sites such as Facebook, Twitter, Instagram, and the rising use of image sharing apps such as Snapchat[8] and dating apps such as Tinder have made it child's play for

---

[6]Strassberg, D. S., McKinnon, R. K., SustaÁta, M. A., & Rullo, J. (2013). Sexting by high school students: An exploratory and descriptive study. Archives of sexual behavior, 42(1), 15–21.

[7]An article in Rolling Stone chronicles the story of Audrie, and shows how sexting can lead to horrifying consequences.
http://www.rollingstone.com/culture/news/sexting-shame-and-suicide–20130917

[8]Snapchat is an image messaging app which destroys messages and images sent after a preset time, usually 10 seconds. It is very popular with

teenagers to exchange pornographic images and sexually explicit images of themselves with each other.

The relatively anonymous and "behind-the-screen" nature of such apps (where you can create fake profiles and upload any photo of yourself) makes it straightforward for boys to chat with several girls. Conversations can turn sexual swiftly, with boys asking girls questions such as, "Do you like to suck dick?", or requesting for nude photos. The problem is that sometimes teenagers are unable to draw the line and go too far, sharing content which, once out there, they have no control over.

The biggest problems come about when teenagers and children start taking inappropriate photos or videos of themselves and posting them on their social network accounts. Such sharing can easily go viral as their friends forward them on to one another. In essence, such apps make sharing so easy that child porn can be accessed by their peers on their iPhones in school. In a well publicised case, six Pennsylvania high school students were charged for child pornography.[9] Three teenage girls took semi-nude pictures of themselves on their cell phones and sent it to their male friends. The girls were charged with manufacturing, disseminating or possessing child pornography, while the boys were charged with possession.

Aside from the legal debate over whether such prosecution of minors is justified, it is also important to ask whether the easy

---

teenagers, and about 200 million messages a day are sent, or about 23 thousand images a second.

[9]Brunker, M. (2009). 'Sexting'surprise: Teens face child porn charges. MSNBC Jan, 15.

availability of porn these days is emboldening teenage boys to request for sexually explicit images or videos from their friends. While there has not been much research done on this subject, one would expect that porn contributes to an unrealistic view of sexuality and is likely to be a big contributor to the trend of sexting.

Protecting our children

Parents, teachers, and caretakers should recognize the extent of the problem of porn in the lives of our children, understand how porn is particularly harmful to our youth, and devise strategies to mitigate the trauma and damage that porn can cause. Porn upsets children at a fundamental level, and confuses their development. It has been demonstrated to lead to earlier sexual involvement, and normalizes non-mainstream sex acts, even leading to sexual violence and abuse.

At the most basic level, parents, teachers, and caretakers should take proactive steps to establish some level of control over the internet browsing habits of our young. For example, parents can consider installing family friendly internet browsers on their children's smartphones. Such browsers intelligently block out known pornographic websites as well as filter for keywords which might indicate inappropriate content, and are useful for both family use as well as for porn addicts. A full descriptive list of the best family filters and software is given later in the Appendix.

Porn harms children

Given that adolescents and children today access the internet on a daily basis, and that the usage of smartphones and tablets is becoming more common among our young, it is likely that most internet access by the younger is portable and unlikely to be monitored effectively. The trend of sexting illustrates this idea perfectly, since parents can be totally unaware of what is shared.

As parents cannot possibly completely control or monitor the browsing habits of their children, it is even more important to educate our children on the potential harm of porn on the internet. Through meaningful engagement with our children on topics of human sexuality, we can prepare them to cope properly with the inadvertent consumption of porn when it happens, and discourage them from deliberately seeking out porn. With regular communication, parents, teachers and caretakers can minimize the likelihood that those in their care are harmed by porn.

We should discuss with our children the appropriate ways to deal with sexts they receive. They should be aware that sending out explicit images of themselves should never be done, and not only because it is illegal. They should be made to understand that anything shared online immediately falls out of their control, and might cause an incredible amount of pain and distress for them.

A simple rule they should follow is to never share anything they do not want seen on a website anyone can access. Further, they should be told of the legal consequences of forwarding any sexts they receive. The only appropriate response is to delete

41

these messages and tell the sender to stop sending such messages again.

Chapter 3

Porn harms its performers

The trends towards themes of degradation and perversion in porn is especially harmful to the people who act in porn videos. This chapter explores the harmful effects of what performers in the porn industry endure. Beyond mere physical maltreatment, performers frequently suffer long lasting psychological damage, shame and guilt. Apart from the serious health risks that come from being a sex performer, many porn actors and actresses turn to addictions such as drugs in order to cope with the abuse, which destroys their bodies and minds. They are also unable to sustain normal intimate relationships.

Physical harm

As the majority of porn is typically geared towards the male consumer, porn typically depicts scenes where males hold sexual control and power over females. As a result porn is especially hateful and harmful to its female performers, who have to endure violence and sexual abuse during video shoots. This is likely to worsen as porn producers explore even harder and more perverse themes in order to hold the attention of their consumers, who have gradually become desensitized to what is currently available. In fact, porn producers themselves admit that they have no choice but to produce more extreme and hardcore videos these days because their customers are no longer satisfied with softcore porn.

Porn has always presented women as objects for males to use for sexual pleasure, but it might not be easy for someone who have not seen porn to understand how violent porn can be today. Female porn performers routinely get physically and verbally abused during filming. They are choked, slapped, and punched during such films, while being abusively handled by their male partners and repeatedly called "bitch", "slut", "whore", or worse.

The sex portrayed by porn is also decidedly non-mainstream and extreme. Anal sex is a regular fixture, and it is common to find porn videos of women being penetrated vaginally, anally, and orally by three men at the same time. Other scenes that are typical include throat-gagging, where a male thrusts his penis so deeply into a female's mouth that she chokes and even vomits; ass-gaping where the male (or males) stretches the female's anus and penetrates her with sex toys or more than one penis; and ass-to-mouth, where the female performs oral sex immediately after anal sex without washing the penis first. In some cases, fecal matter can be seen, which adds to the humiliation of the female.

Such scenes usually end with a money shot of the male (or males) ejaculating on the female's body, typically the face since it most directly shows the power dynamic between the male and the female who is submissively kneeling down in front of the male. As a result of facial ejaculations, female porn performers frequently develop conjunctivitis in their eyes.

A study analyzed 304 videos and found that 88.2 percent of scenes contained physical violence, principally spanking, gagging, and slapping, while 48.7 percent of these scenes contained verbal attack, mainly name calling.[1] It further found that the aggressors were mainly males. Females were typically the targets, and displayed pleasure or responded neutrally to aggression, which encouraged further abuse and violence. This suggests that physical and verbal abuse is the norm rather than the exception in porn.

A former porn performer describes her experience of how violent it can get in the porn industry:[2]

> Donkey Punch was the most brutal, depressing, scary scene that I have ever done. I have tried to block it out of my memory due to the severe

---

[1]Bridges, A. J., Wosnitzer, R., Scharrer, E., Sun, C., & Liberman, R. (2010). Aggression and sexual behavior in best-selling pornography videos: A content analysis update. Violence Against Women, 16(10), 1065–1085.

[2]http://www.covenanteyes.com/2008/10/29/ex-porn-star-tells-the-truth-part–2/

abuse I received during the filming. The guy, Steve French, has a natural hatred towards women in the sense that he has always been known to be more brutal than EVER needed. I agreed to do the scene thinking it was less beating, except the 'punch' in the head. If you noticed, Steve had worn his solid gold ring the entire time, and continued to punch me with it. I actually stopped the scene while it was being filmed because I was in too much pain.

Even though female porn performers evidently feel pain and are visibly abused in many such scenes, porn attempts to recreate the fantasy that all females actually enjoy such treatment and that males know what they really need or want sexually. For instance, note the suggestion of suffering and the implied enjoyment of the female in a typical description of a porn video:

Hot Blonde Teen Suffers The Deepthroat and The Anal Banging. Hailey has it all to become great in the porn business, she is blonde, skinny, tall, hot and has no problem with anal sex. But still, she didn't performed all that well in this audition. She seemed incapable of handling the big dick and suffered a lot the deepthroat and the anal sex. She did love the cumshot, though.

Porn harms its performers

Jenna Jameson, arguably one of the world's most famous porn actresses, describes the experience of most first time performers in the industry like this in her book:[3]

> Most girls get their first experience in gonzo films—in which they're taken to a crappy studio apartment in Mission Hills and penetrated in every hole possible by some abusive asshole who thinks her name is Bitch. And these girls, some of whom have the potential to become major stars in the industry, go home afterward and pledge never to do it again because it was such a terrible experience. But, unfortunately, they can't take that experience back, so they live the rest of their days in fear that their relatives, their co-workers, or their children will find out, which they inevitably do.

Porn will continue its trend of becoming more sadistic, brutal, and cruel as long as we as a society continue to consume and demand more of it in order to satiate our desensitized sexual desires. Because most of porn is geared towards the male consumer, female performers end up bearing the brunt of the violence in porn. There are many other examples that one can easily find with a simple Google search today, and porn which depicts females as objects deserving of abuse is all too common.

---

[3]Jameson, J., & Strauss, N. (2010). How to make love like a porn star: A cautionary tale. HarperCollins.

Psychological abuse

Apart from the physical abuse that porn performers endure, what is arguably worse is the sense of being used as an object rather than as a human being deserving of dignity. Erin Moore, a former porn performer shares her personal experience: "Over the course of my porn career I have been belittled and treated like a piece of trash more than I could have ever imagined in a lifetime I would. I wasn't a woman in any of these directors eyes, I was nothing to them. The male talent at times were nice, but sometimes, they were horrible. I've had men choke me, slap me, thrust me so hard until I couldn't walk and this would happen even after I would tell them to stop. They have no respect for women."[4]

Porn producers often view porn performers as interchangeable commodities and have no regard for their feelings or wellbeing. During a shoot, female porn performers are entirely at the mercy of the filming crew and director, and frequently do not have a say on what happens. While they might have an initial inkling of what the scene is going to be about, their control vanishes once shooting begins and they have to endure anything that the producers might require from them. For instance, female porn performers might not be able to stop filming even when they take abuse from an overly aggressive male performer. They might be disallowed from cleaning off semen from their faces and asked to put on pretend smiles while the camera rolls. Producers can threaten to withhold payment or ask for damages

---

[4]http://www.oneangrygirl.net/erinmoore.html

when performers refuse to comply, which makes it difficult for them to not comply despite the pain or humiliation.

The loss of autonomy over what happens to their bodies and the way they are treated leads many porn performers to fall into depression and seek out ways of escape. A large percentage of porn performers turn to drugs and alcohol as a way of numbing their emotions, which further compounds their problems as they become addicted and have to continue working in porn to pay for their drug addiction.

Health issues

According to former porn performer Jersey Jaxin, up to 75 percent of the performers in the industry use drugs as a way of dealing with the way they are treated in porn: "The main thing going around now is crystal meth, cocaine and heroin. You have to numb yourself to go on set. The more you work, the more you have to numb yourself. The more you become addicted, the more your personal life is nothing but drugs. Your whole life becomes nothing but porn."[5]

In the Jenna Jameson's book How to Make Love Like a Porn Star, she describes how she spiraled out of control due to her addiction to meth, eventually losing so much weight that she ended up weighing only 80 pounds (36kg). Granted, in the book she did not seek out meth because of abuse she suffered

---

[5]http://www.oneangrygirl.net/jerseyjaxin.html

while shooting porn, but because of the company she was keeping at that time. However, her story points to a broader trend where young women, typically uneducated with few economic options, are lured into the porn industry where the kind of work and the people they associate with push them towards drugs. Drug dealers are motivated to seek out these young women as customers as these women typically have lots of free time, fast access to easy cash, and minimal supervision or positive role models in their lives.

The porn industry typically depicts unprotected sex, because porn producers are worried that the use of condoms would remove an important fantasy component of their product and result in a loss of revenue. According to some estimates, revenues can drop by as much as 30 percent in shoots where condoms are used. One big risk of being a porn performer is that of contracting sexually transmitted diseases (STDs), such as HIV, syphilis, chlamydia, and gonorrhea, among other diseases.

As a group, porn performers have sex more frequently with more sex partners than the general population, and they usually engage in higher risk sexual practices such as anal sex or with multiple partners. They hence have a common incentive to prevent any outbreak of disease. One effective way they do so is through regular testing for STDs every 14 or 28 days. These tests cover HIV, Chlamydia, Gonorrhea, Hepatitis B, and C, as well as a test for Trichomoniasis Vaginalis.

When a performer tests positive, studios that adhere to standards set by the Free Speech Coalition, an industry trade group, will impose a moratorium on all filming until all his/her direct partners and their partners are tested. In August 2013, a performer tested positive for HIV, which triggered a stop in shooting nationwide in the US. Within weeks, three other independent individuals were reported to test positive, prompting a second moratorium on shooting.

While this system has definitely reduced the risk of HIV and other STD transmission, critics argue that porn performers are still subject to a high residual level of risk as long as they do not use direct prevention methods such as condoms. According to Michael Weinstein, president of the AIDS Healthcare Foundation, they can still transmit STDs in the period between testing. He said, "If you think that Russian roulette is a great way to protect workers, then the present system is perfect."

Rod Daily and Cameron Bay, both porn performers who tested positive for HIV in September 2013, have argued that condom use should be used for all porn shoots, and suggest that the porn industry is inherently risky. The New York Post quoted Bay describing a shoot where "an actor working with her cut himself and was allowed to continue filming an explicit scene even though Daily, who was on set that day, would have stood in for him."[6]

---

[6]http://nypost.com/2013/09/19/hiv-infected-porn-stars-call-for-condom-use/

Relationship harm

Porn performers typically also face immense difficulties maintaining intimate romantic relationships in their lives.

In Jenna Jameson's book, she shared her own difficulties getting into close relationships with men because of the emotional complications of dating a porn performer. In one episode of her life, she was in a committed long term relationship with a man, and had already decided to stop filming boy-girl scenes. However, due to contractual obligations, she had one final video to shoot. Predictably, this distressed her partner immensely. The filming of this video led to an enormous fight where he called her a "whore". According to her, "It takes a certain kind of man to be able to live with the fact that the woman he loves has sex with other man on camera for a living. And I haven't met that man yet."

What happens in reality is that some female performers end up dating their agents or managers, who are only in the relationship to take advantage of the cash making ability of their girlfriends.

It is almost impossible for male porn performers to form relationships with women. While a female performer might film about ten scenes a year, a male performer has to do at least seven to ten scenes a week. No woman would ever be comfortable being in a relationship with a male who has sex with seven other women once a week, and even female performers are wary of getting into a relationship with them as it would be bad for their career to only be able to have sex with him on camera.

Porn harms its performers

In certain cases where male and female performers pair off, they might eventually grow so close that either one or the other would be unwilling to let their partner shoot videos with other people. This typically ends their career as they are taken off the market, or leads to severe emotional pain when one or the other decides that he or she is unwilling to commit to the relationship and would rather continue to remain in the industry.

Part II

How to go porn free

Chapter 4

Do I have a porn addiction?

Addiction is a tricky subject to tackle, since it involves the admission to ourselves that we have a problem. In this chapter, we will provide some useful pointers for you to 1) determine if you have an addiction to porn, 2) identify the triggers that are likely to lead you to consume porn, and 3) identify some strategies that you can adopt to deal with your addiction.

A person's initial attraction to porn stems from its ability to arouse him sexually and to stimulate his curiosity. It further stimulates his natural sexual appetite to want to see more and more. Internet porn makes it particularly easy for us to do this, as it presents a continuous dizzying array of fresh videos and images for us to consume. Before long, as we described earlier in Chapter One, soft core images no longer "do it" for us, and we turn to more hard core images as our brains get rewired. This kind of addiction can be termed physical addiction, and it should be distinguished from an addiction that is psychological in nature. Although we can argue that the brain is merely physically affected by our consumption of porn, prolonged or intense use of violent hardcore porn also affects us on a deeper psychological level when the brain undergoes even more profound changes. This can be seen particularly in cases of young people, where exposure to porn disrupts their sexual development process, leading to severe psychological problems.

For a quick test of whether you are indeed addicted to porn, simply try to stop consuming porn for a couple of days, and observe the changes in your mood and motivation to consume porn again. What you experience personally will tell you a lot of the degree to which you are addicted. The following will attempt to shed some light on why some people are more likely to succeed in stopping their porn addiction without much effort and why some are unable to do so, despite repeated attempts.

To do so, it is important to have a discussion on whether you are only physically addicted to porn or also psychologically addicted. Physical addiction is easier to manage and overcome, as evidenced by the tens of thousands of people who have reported stopping their addiction to porn once they found out how it was harming them. It is roughly similar to a smoker in the process of quitting. After an initial uncomfortable period of detoxification, the smoker finds himself feeling much better without the need to smoke. However, many smokers find themselves unable to quit because they also have a psychological need to smoke to deal with, for example, a stressful work environment.

Do I have a porn addiction?

When I was serving in the army, I observed that many people picked up smoking, especially during the tough training periods. This was because they were facing a difficult situation (away from family, intense training, military discipline) and used smoking as a way to physically deal with their loss of control. A study of 943 US Army enlistees leaving Vietnam in 1971 illustrates this well.[1] Half of them represented the general sample of all enlistees who did not test drug positive at the time they left for Vietnam. Before arrival at Vietnam, they were basically non drug users, and less than one percent had ever been addicted to narcotics. During their service in Vietnam, almost half of them tried narcotics, and a full one fifth of them became addicted. After they returned from Vietnam, their use of drugs and addiction levels returned to pretty much pre-Vietnam levels. Why was this so? During the war, they had a physical need to deal with their situation by using drugs. This need essentially evaporated once they were out of the war. Having no prior psychological need to take drugs, they could stop once they returned home and the physical trigger was no longer present in their lives.

A person can deal with a physical addiction to porn by simply making a determined decision to stop. Based on anecdotes, what is known as a "reboot", a process of restoring your brain to normal functioning by refraining from porn and masturbation, typically takes about two to four months.

---

[1]Robins, L. N., Helzer, J. E., & Davis, D. H. (1975). Narcotic use in Southeast Asia and afterward: An interview study of 898 Vietnam returnees. Archives of General Psychiatry, 32(8), 955.

Although it sounds simple, in practice many people relapse along the way, as addictions usually also have a psychological aspect, which you will have to deal with in order to ensure a complete end to your porn addiction. An addiction with psychological aspects arise when a person starts to use porn as a stand in for something else in his/her life, such as to deal with negative moods or as a response to stress.

However, it is often difficult to say with certainty in what way has porn developed a psychological hold on any single individual as human sexuality is complex. Nonetheless, some indicators of a psychological addiction may include violent sexual fantasies, irritability when one is unable to access porn, or increased porn consumption during stressful periods.

As each individual is different, it would be useful for you to be especially mindful of the unique psychological triggers which lead you to consume porn instead of just making a determined decision not to touch porn, which often only works well when someone's addiction is purely physical in nature.

The following section will help you identify typical physical and psychological triggers which lead a person to give in to their porn addiction.

Chapter 5

Triggers

Triggers are situations or circumstances which first plant the idea of consuming porn in our minds. For instance, a simple trigger may be a screen popup on our browser of a porn image, which invites us to further click on to see more. Identifying what triggers us to first think of going to porn is important as it allows us to deal with the trigger at the moment it presents itself. In practice, this is not as obvious as it seems, as many of the situations which trigger a person to eventually consume porn when no one is watching can be very subtle and may even work without the person being fully conscious of what happened.

We shall discuss two levels of triggers: 1) environmental triggers, and 2) situational triggers.

Environmental triggers are easy to identify and obvious, while situational triggers have a psychological aspect and may be difficult to detect even by the person himself.

Environmental triggers precede the actual act of porn consumption quickly or even immediately, while the time between a situational trigger and porn consumption can take from hours to days.

Environmental triggers

A person is most likely to consume porn when they are physically alone in a room at a time when no one is likely to disturb them. This is the most obvious trigger that one should be aware of. When a person consumes porn they do not do it at work but at home most of the time. Similarly, married husbands who consume porn would generally not do it in the same room as their wife, and perhaps retreat into the study to do so. Parents should not be surprised that their teenage children are spending hours consuming porn when they lock themselves up in their rooms, saying they want private space.

This works simply because the force of habit and/or a repeated familiar situation leads a person to associate it with consuming porn. For example, a person who visits porn websites at night just before sleeping does so because the environment is conducive to surfing porn. Just by being in that same place and time everyday will be a strong enough trigger for that person to be "reminded" that it is time to consume porn.

In short, there are certain places and times when you are most likely to consume porn. This makes dealing with environmental triggers straightforward. It should not be difficult to come up with a list of places or times when you might be most likely to consume porn, and limit your exposure to such triggers. For instance, the family computer may be placed in a room which the whole family can enter freely: say the living room or a main study room. If you consume porn mainly at home and you are motivated to control your addiction to porn, you can consider installing internet filters, which is discussed below in the Appendix. If you mainly consume porn at night, you will have a much higher chance of controlling your addiction if you do not even start using the computer once it gets late.

A related trigger would be accidental exposure to an explicit image. This can happen inadvertently online sometimes, which can cause one to think of porn and masturbation. It can be dealt with in similar ways as above, as it is likely that a person would only be triggered to consume porn and masturbate in a private place, for instance, and not at work.

Situational triggers

While the environment where a person consumes porn regularly matters, it would be useful to consider if they are any prior acts and situations that would precipitate the thought of consuming porn even before a location of convenience and privacy arose.

For the sake of illustration, consider the example of John. While at work, his boss tells him that he has to complete a report by the end of the day before he can return home. He originally planned to have dinner with his wife at home, but it seems impossible now. He does not see a choice, and ends up working till late in the night before going home to complete his report. At home, he finishes his report only to find that his family is already asleep. Alone at the computer, he decides to check out some porn sites to end off the day. In this case, it is not so clear cut that it was merely the location and timing that triggered him to act on his porn addiction.

The situational trigger came earlier in the day at the moment when John actually realized he had to stay late at work. This may or may not have been a conscious thought. He perhaps just said to himself something like "well at least I'll have a chance to look at porn when I get home tonight". Or it could have been a more indirect thought, where he merely took some relief in the fact that he would probably have more time to himself when he got home that night. Since it was during private moments at home late at night when he usually consumed porn on his computer, the mere thought of having this time alone at night would have been sufficient for him to unconsciously decide that he would be doing just so.

Any stressful situation can lead to emotions, thoughts, or acts leading to addictive porn consumption, and it is important for a person to identify such situations at the moment when they arise, if they are to consciously and effectively deal with the issue. In John's case, he could have realized that he was likely to surf porn after finishing his work on his home desktop, and instead decide consciously to finish everything at the office before going home, where he would just go straight to bed. By identifying the higher likelihood of him acting on his porn addiction because of the added stress of extra work into the late hours, he could have taken steps in advance to prevent himself from giving into his addiction later at night.

What are some of the triggers which would lead a person to consume porn? The general categories of stressors today for most of us would be work or school, family or relationships, and our finances. These triggers are highly personal and vary from person to person. What would apply to someone else may not apply to you. The main idea is that a person addicted to porn should be mindful that any potentially stressful situation which comes up (either emotionally, physically, or mentally) may lead to a conscious decision or unconscious rationalization to consume porn. Even if the consumption takes place hours or days later, we can say that the decision to do so occurred the moment the situational trigger took place.

Situational triggers work on a psychological level, and are more difficult to identify than a convenient place to consume porn or an accidental explicit image seen online. Hence it is important that we make an extra effort to identify such triggers. Having a psychological element, they are also critical in explaining why a person who seemed to have successfully controlled their porn addiction might relapse.

Consider the experience of John. He managed to go porn free for a few weeks, and was feeling great. However, he recently started consuming porn on his computer again, and did not understand why exactly he did so. It turned out that the annual peak period of his company recently started, and he had to spend more time at work under greater stress to perform. He started to use his computer at night at home to cope with his additional workload, and decided one night to just take a "peek" at some porn online.

An understanding that the increased stress at work could have situationally triggered him to relapse would have been very helpful for Jack. When his workload started to increase, he could have identified that as a situational trigger which increased the chances of him consuming porn. He could have then made specific plans not to do so. In this case, it was not so much of any environmental triggers which prompted his relapse. Instead, it was against the background of a stressful situational trigger which amplified the likelihood of his porn addiction resurfacing. Without such an understanding, it would have been confusing and disappointing for Jack each time he unsuccessfully tried to control his porn addiction.

Chapter 6

Strategies and tactics to deal with porn

Dealing with a porn addiction can be difficult, as a person needs to undo the physical and psychological changes resulting from porn consumption. In this section, we shall discuss some useful strategies and relevant tactics that a person can use to deal with his/her porn addiction.

Cold turkey (aka reboot)

A popular method encouraged by the NoFap internet community[1] ("fapping" as slang for masturbation) is to simply stop

---

[1]NoFap.org is made up of more than 90,000 members who are dedicated to give up porn and masturbation in hopes of improving their lives.

masturbation and porn consumption completely. Interestingly, they have a "Hard Mode", where a person attempts to completely avoid sex, even with a real sexual partner.

This works by giving the brain a chance to heal itself from the rewiring that porn causes, which would allow a person to regain normal functioning of their sensory faculties for pleasure. As explained earlier, porn consumption causes a person's pleasure receptors to shut down in the brain, which causes him to require more and more visual sexual stimulation to experience the same amount of pleasure.

According to nofap.org, a successful reboot/detoxification period can take about 2 to 4 months, which is similar to that of drug addiction. In a study of cocaine addiction, significant dopamine receptors can persist 3 to 4 months after detoxification.[2] What this means is that it is possible to reverse most physical harm resulting from porn after a dedicated period of complete self-restraint.

Once the harms of porn consumption is clear, there is usually enough determination for a person to deal with his/her physical addiction to porn. However, it may be difficult for an individual to complete the program of complete abstinence after a prolonged period of addiction if one has psychological issues of dependence on porn. Hence, one should be alert to

---

[2]Volkow, N. D., Fowler, J. S., Wang, G. J., Hitzemann, R., Logan, J., Schlyer, D. J., ... & Wolf, A. P. (1993). Decreased dopamine D2 receptor availability is associated with reduced frontal metabolism in cocaine abusers. Synapse, 14(2), 169–177.

how external situations may affect one's resolve to completely stop their porn habit.

There are several tactics that you must adopt in order to have a successful reboot.

You should remove all possible environmental triggers of porn. This would include disposing all pornographic materials in your house, permanently deleting all porn from your computer and devices, and blocking internet porn using tools such as web filters and DNS filtering (a full list of online resources are available in the Appendix). DNS filtering at the network level will block porn on every device which is connected to the network. If you consume porn mainly on a desktop, move the desktop out from a private room if possible. If you consume porn on a portable laptop, stop using it completely at times you usually consume porn. If you consume porn on a mobile, ensure that porn websites are filtered at the level of the wireless network.

Once you have done this, you can focus on identifying the situational triggers which would make you more likely to consume porn. For instance, a quarrel between you and your partner might lead to you seeking out porn a few hours later.

Take a moment to think through some of the potential situations which would increase the likelihood of you giving in to your porn addiction, and write them down. As discussed earlier, this might lead you to consider situations which you previously did not think to identify as the key moment which eventually led you to consume porn. As porn addictions have a psychological component as well, it is important that you complete this mental and writing exercise so that you will be more aware of your own psychology and how that can affect your behavior.

Community and accountability

Having community support is also crucial in dealing with your addiction to porn. You can choose between joining an online community on nofap.org, or a face to face community, such as a church group. What is important is that you are able to find a group of like-minded people who have gone through or are going through the same issues as you. By having community support, you will benefit from increased accountability and the sense that you are not going through this phase alone by yourself.

Accountability is the willingness to accept responsibility and account for one's action, and is influential in determining if you will be successful in controlling your addiction. As a wise man once said, "As iron sharpens iron, so one person sharpens another."[3] If nobody knows about your porn addiction it is likely that you will fail again and again.

I would recommend that you find an accountability partner on NoFap's website at http://www.nofap.org/forum/forumdisplay.php?7-Accountability-Partners immediately. After posting a short thread on the forum, a couple of people will request to be your accountability partner. After you agree to

---

[3]Proverbs 27:17 (New International Version)

enter into an accountability relationship with someone, you can regularly check in with each other on how you are doing through a channel you are most comfortable with, such as by phone, email, or text message.

If you are already part of a community which regularly meets up (such as a church, work, or school group), you can also consider asking someone in that group to be your accountability partner. This may be better if you can find someone you are comfortable sharing your struggles with as you can regularly meet up face to face with them. For married people, you may also consider enlisting your spouse's support and help as your accountability partner.

For even more accountability, you can consider using a service called Covenant Eyes. It's an internet service which automatically generates a report of your internet surfing habits and sends them to the people you want to be accountable to. It is a bit pricey, but may work in cases where you feel that you require even more accountability.

A few more things about accountability. You should decide to be totally honest before you enter into any accountability relationship with someone. There will be instances where you will feel the impulse to hide something which you feel you will be judged for, but this will defeat the purpose of having an accountability partner in the first place.

You should be aware that there may be consequences to being totally honest with someone. If you are concerned that an accountability partner is going to be judgmental or unable to maintain confidentiality, you may decide to find an accountability partner online, where there is a higher degree of anonymity.

To sum up, the best way to quit porn is to go cold turkey, removing all possible environmental triggers and becoming aware of the situations which may trigger you to consume porn. To help you along your way, you should get someone along on the journey with you. All the best!

Online resources

There are many online tools today that can protect you and your loved ones from porn.

For home

At home, one good way to filter most porn websites is OpenDNS Family Shield. After changing some simple settings once on your computer or home router, all devices in your home would be good to go. Visit http://www.opendns.com/ home-solutions/parental-controls/and click on OpenDNS Family Shield -> Sign Up Now and follow the easy to understand instructions. If you set up the filtering on your home wireless router, all devices connected to your home network automatically benefit from the family filter.

K9 Web Protection, once installed on your computer, will allow you to block all porn sites.

If you are using the Chrome or Firefox browser, you can install Metacert's Metasurf add ons for these browsers, which will block most adult content effectively.

Covenant Eyes is an internet service which provides both internet filtering and an accountability report, which summarizes a person's internet browsing history and flags out any potentially pornographic content. This is useful for added accountability with your accountability partner, and also for parents to safely monitor the browsing habits of their children. Covenant Eyes also provide browsers for Apple and Android devices, and internet usage from these mobile devices will show up in a single accountability report.

Links

- http://www.opendns.com/home-solutions/parental-controls/

- http://www1.k9webprotection.com/aboutk9/overview

- https://metacert.com

- http://www.covenanteyes.com/services/internet-accountability/

Mobile devices

For your mobile devices, you should consider installing special browsers for you and especially for your children, who are likely to inadvertently look at porn otherwise.

On Android devices, you can install Metacert's free software, which will provide filtering against explicit content, as well as control the times at which different apps can be used.

On Apple devices such as the iPhone and iPad, I would recommend that you disable the regular Safari browser, and install either the browser from K9 Web Protection, or Metacert's Olly browser. In order to disable Safari, go to the Settings App, and click to General, and then Restrictions. After you enter a restriction four digit password, toggle the slider for Safari to disable it.

The default Safari browser on Apple devices may not be the best way to filter for explicit content. However, if you wish to do so, you can set website restrictions under the Settings app by clicking General -> Restrictions. After you enter a restriction four digit password, you can set what content is allowed. It is recommended that you restrict access to adult content by going to Websites -> Limit Adult Content. Under those settings, you may further manually block any website.

Links

- https://metacert.com/android

- https://itunes.apple.com/us/app/k9-web-protection-browser/id407657840?mt=8

- https://itunes.apple.com/us/app/metacert-safe-browser-parental/id556938946?mt=8

Online communities

Reddit has a vibrant forum (http://www.reddit.com/r/NoFap/) for people trying to overcome their "PMO" (porn, masturbation, orgasm) addiction. They call themselves "fapstronauts", and the community is friendly and open. You can share your own personal stories and strategies on how to fight the urge to seek out porn.

NoFap.org is the sister website of reddit's community. It's another online community which features a forum and challenges visitors to "Join the movement for self improvement". To find an accountability partner, visit their forums at http://www.nofap.org/forum/forumdisplay.php?7-Accountability-Partners.

Printed in Great Britain
by Amazon.co.uk, Ltd.,
Marston Gate.